LET'S
DANCE

BALLET

Aaron Carr

www.av2books.com

LET'S READ AV² BY WEIGL™
ADDED VALUE • AUDIO VISUAL

Go to **www.av2books.com**, and enter this book's unique code.

BOOK CODE

L 9 2 3 6 3 3

AV² by Weigl brings you media enhanced books that support active learning.

AV² provides enriched content that supplements and complements this book. Weigl's AV² boo strive to create inspired learning and engage young minds in a total learning experience.

Your AV² Media Enhanced books come alive with...

Audio
Listen to sections of the book read aloud.

Video
Watch informative video clips.

Embedded Weblinks
Gain additional information for research.

Try This!
Complete activities and hands-on experiments.

Key Words
Study vocabulary, and complete a matching word activity.

Quizzes
Test your knowledge.

Slide Show
View images and captions, and prepare a presentation.

... and much, much more

Published by AV² by Weigl
350 5th Avenue, 59th Floor
New York, NY 10118

Website: www.av2books.com   www.weigl.com

Library of Congress Control Number: 2013941095
ISBN 978-1-48961-747-7 (hardcover)
ISBN 978-1-48961-748-4 (softcover)

Printed in the United States of America in North Mankato, Minnesota
1 2 3 4 5 6 7 8 9 0   17 16 15 14 13

052013
WEP220513

Project Coordinator: Jason McClure   Designer: Mandy Christiansen

Weigl acknowledges Alamy, Dreamstime, and Getty Images as the primary image suppliers for this title.

LET'S DANCE

BALLET

CONTENTS

I love ballet dancing.
I am going to dance today.

Ballet dancing is more than 600 years old.

I dress for ballet.
I wear a black body suit
and pink tights.

6

Ballet Style

Ballet dancers must wear a special outfit.

I wear special ballet shoes.
Ballet shoes are like slippers.

Fancy Feet

Older dancers may wear shoes with split soles.

I take ballet classes at a dance studio. The studio is a big room with smooth floors.

Mirrors let ballet dancers see how they move.

I stretch before class starts. This helps me get ready to dance.

Ballet dancers use a barre when they stretch.

I watch my teacher do a dance move. Then I try to do it the same way.

14

Ballet Moves

Ballet has five basic moves.

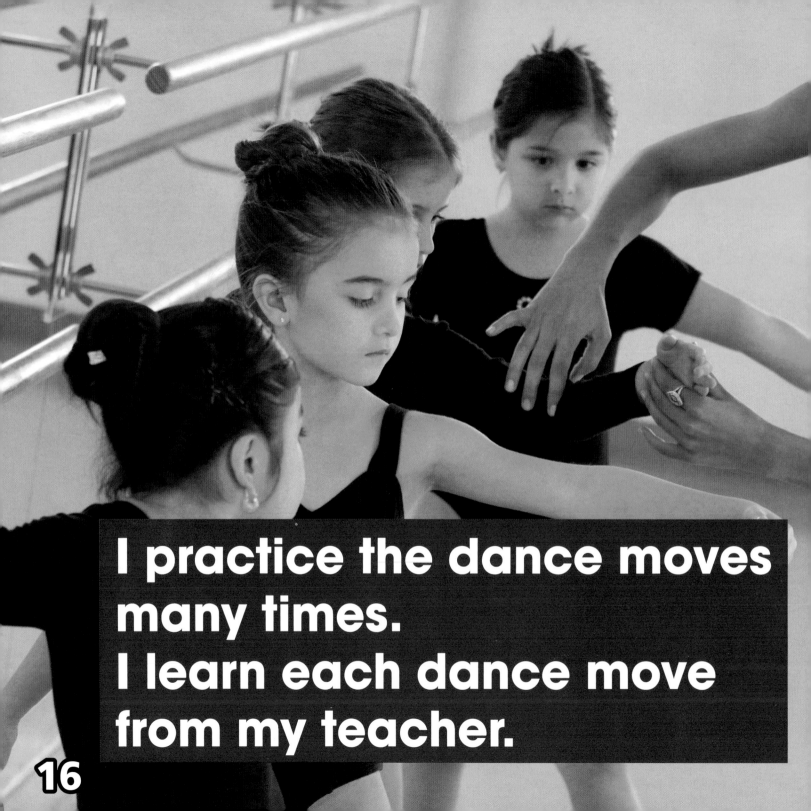

I practice the dance moves many times.
I learn each dance move from my teacher.

Ballet Work

Learning each move takes hours of practice.

My class puts on a ballet show. We all dance the same moves at the same time.

Ballet shows are called recitals.

Ballet dancing helps me stay healthy.
I love ballet dancing.

ST. JOHN THE BAPTIST PARISH LIBRARY
2920 NEW HIGHWAY
LAPLACE, LOUISIANA

21

BALLET FACTS

These pages provide more detail about the interesting facts found in the book. They are intended to be used by adults as a learning support to help young readers round out their knowledge of each style of dance featured in the *Let's Dance* series.

Pages 4–5

Getting Ready Ballet is one of the most popular forms of dance. It was invented in the 1400s in Italy. Since then, ballet has inspired many other dance styles, including jazz and modern dance. For this reason, many dance teachers recommend that beginning dancers learn ballet first. Once they know ballet, they will be better prepared to learn other styles of dance.

Pages 6–7

What I Wear Most ballet schools have a dress code for dancers. Girls often must wear navy blue or black body suits, pink tights, and ballet slippers. Girls with long hair wear their hair up in a tight bun. Boys generally wear white T-shirts or tank tops, black shorts or pants, and black ballet slippers. However, some ballet schools may have less strict dress codes.

Pages 8–9

What I Need Ballet slippers are light-weight and flexible dance shoes. They can be made from leather, canvas, or satin. Young dancers wear shoes with a full sole. Older dancers can wear split-soled shoes. These shoes have a gap in the sole under the arch of the foot. This allows for better flexibility. Advanced ballet dancers wear pointe shoes, which let the dancers dance on the tips of their toes.

Pages 10–11

Where I Dance Dance studios are often large and open rooms. This allows dancers plenty of space to move around. Studios usually have sprung floors. This means the floors are flexible. A flexible floor lessens the impact dancers feel when performing jumps and other high-impact dance moves. At least one wall in a studio is covered with mirrors. The mirrors allow dancers to check their form.

I stretch before class starts. This helps me get ready to dance.

Ballet Fact

Ballet dancers use a barre when they stretch.

Warming Up It is important to stretch before and after dancing. Stretching lowers the risk of injury. Ballet dancers do a variety of stretches for their legs, arms, and torso. They often use a barre to help them stretch their legs. A barre is a horizontal rail that is usually attached to one wall of the dance studio. Dancers will lift one of their legs onto the barre to stretch their leg muscles.

I watch my teacher do a dance move. Then I try to do it the same way.

Ballet Moves

Ballet has five basic moves.

Learning the Moves Dance classes feature one or more teachers. The teachers demonstrate the positions and movements to the students and help the students repeat the moves. In ballet, there are five basic positions that all beginning dancers must learn. They are numbered from first position to fifth position. Each position involves different ways of standing and placing the feet.

I practice the dance moves many times. I learn each dance move from my teacher.

Ballet Work

Learning each move takes hours of practice.

Practicing Practice is very important in learning ballet. Even the five basic positions take hours of practice to learn properly. As dancers advance, the moves become more challenging and the amount of practice needed increases. For most dance schools, beginning dancers have one class each week. Older dancers may have several classes each week.

My class puts on a ballet show. We all dance the same moves at the same time.

Show Time

Ballet shows are called recitals.

Show Time Most dance schools have one or two recitals each year, with one at Christmas and one in spring or summer. At a recital, students perform a routine they have practiced. They perform the routine to music, and often wear special costumes. Family and friends come to see the show and support the dancers. It is considered bad luck to wish a dancer good luck before a performance. Instead, people say "break a leg."

Ballet dancing helps me stay healthy. I love ballet dancing.

Staying Healthy Like all forms of physical activity, ballet is an excellent way to stay active and healthy. Practicing ballet promotes physical fitness, flexibility, and good posture. In order to get the greatest benefit from ballet, it is important to eat healthy foods, such as fruits, vegetables, and whole grains. Healthy foods provide the body with the energy it needs to perform well.

KEY WORDS

Research has shown that as much as 65 percent of all written material published in English is made up of 300 words. These 300 words cannot be taught using pictures or learned by sounding them out. They must be recognized by sight. This book contains 55 common sight words to help young readers improve their reading fluency and comprehension. This book also teaches young readers several important content words. These words are paired with pictures to aid in learning and improve understanding.

Page	Sight Words First Appearance	Page	Content Words First Appearance
4	am, I, to	4	ballet dancing
5	is, more, old, than, years	5	fact
6	a, and, for	6	body suit, tights
7	must	7	dancers, outfit, style
8	are, like	8	shoes, slippers
9	feet, may, with	9	soles
10	at, big, take, the	10	ballet classes, floors, room, studio
11	how, let, look, move, see, they	11	mirrors
12	before, get, helps, me, this	13	barre
13	use, when	14	teacher
14	do, it, my, same, then, try, watch, way	17	hours
15	has	19	recitals
16	each, from, learn, many, times		
17	of, work		
18	all, on, puts, show, we		

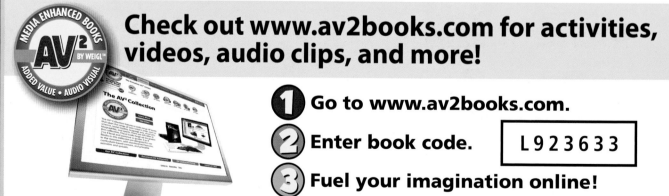